For Alfie, a good dog

This edition published in Great Britain by
Ravette Publishing Limited 2014
PO Box 876, Horsham, West Sussex RH12 9GH
www.ravettepublishing.tel

ISBN: 978-1-84161-386-4

JEFF'S DOG

-Diary of a bad dog-

by Allan Plenderleith

It wasn't so much the poo in the slipper that bothered Jeff, more the smirk on the dog's face.

The dog had told Ginger
the cat flap was the one on the right.

It's true what they say - after years together, dogs and their owners begin to share the same behaviour.

Clearly the dog had figured out
how to work E-BAY.

The dog had made the mistake of licking Lily's feet after a hard day's shopping.

Once again, someone had sharpened the strings on Jeff's guitar.

The dog was serious - Maude's lap
belonged to him and him only.

The dog was thrilled - Jeff had left him a curry on the floor, and it was warm.

The dog had noticed Jeff no longer required the company of ladies, not since he had begun drinking beer.

Dug was surprised when, during love-making, Barbara began tickling his bum.

Jeff's dog was so embarrassed -
it was cold and Alf was staring at
Lily's nipples again.

Jeff's dog soon learned to stay
clear of romantic cuddles by the fire.

The new retractable lead seemed to be
a tad on the powerful side.

Whilst giving the dog emergency
mouth to mouth, Jeff blows a bit too hard.

Having stopped for a quick wee in the park, Jeff was delighted when Maude gave him a special surprise.

The dog didn't recognise
his owner ever since she got
buttox injections.

The dog had given the cat some tips
on how to cover up his poo properly.

The dog had told Jeff that for her
birthday Maude wanted something
with loads of diamonds.

Losing the keys and getting stuck in the cat flap, were only the beginning of Jeff's problems that day.

Although annoyed that the dog had
eaten her homework, Moira was secretly
impressed when he got it right.

Jeff decides never again to let the dog
eat the leftover vindaloo.

Jeff's dog soon learned not to
stick his head out of the car window
when it was moving.

Jeff finally accepts it's time to take the dog out for a walk.

Although shocking at the time, later everyone agreed that the dog farting itself into the fire was actually bloody hilarious.

The dog took his favourite romantic partner out for a meal.

Surprisingly knowledgeable for a dog, Jeff's dog had told Maude how to put her digital photos on the mantelpiece.

Jeff's dog was so embarrassed
by his owner's old mobile.

Jeff's dog had told Dug that when out with your friends you should put your money in a kitty.

Jeff plays that popular party game
'Guess the real Walnut Whip'.

Jeff liked it when the dog slept
on the bed because of the lovely warm
feeling he got through the duvet.

After repeated banging and a loud
crack, Jeff's door finally closed.

The dog had discovered running on
newly polished floors was not a good idea.

Jeff's dog discovers the new sofa
was not fire retardant.

Unfortunately it was only after their rampant bed action, that they realised the dog was under the bed.

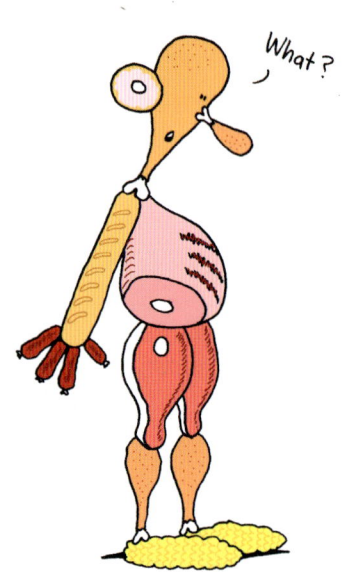

Jeff hadn't realised he'd forgotten
to feed the dog.

Jeff's dog was about to become the
ill-fated star of a You've Been Framed clip.

Other ODD SQUAD gift books available …

	ISBN	PRICE
The Odd Squad's Kama Sutra **(new)**	978-1-84161-385-7	£5.99
Cartoons to Cheer up a Grumpy Old Git	978-1-84161-360-4	£4.99
Cartoons to Cheer up a Stroppy Mare	978-1-84161-361-1	£4.99
I Love Beer	978-1-84161-238-6	£5.99
I Love Dad	978-1-84161-252-2	£5.99
I Love Mum	978-1-84161-249-2	£5.99
I Love Poo	978-1-84161-240-9	£5.99
I Love Sex	978-1-84161-241-6	£4.99
I Love Wine	978-1-84161-239-3	£4.99
I Love Xmas	978-1-84161-262-1	£4.99

HOW TO ORDER:

Please send a cheque/postal order in £ sterling, made payable to 'Ravette Publishing' for the cover price of the book/s and allow the following for post & packing …

UK & BFPO	70p for the first book & 40p per book thereafter
Europe & Eire	£1.30 for the first book & 70p per book thereafter
Rest of the world	£2.20 for the first book & £1.10 per book thereafter

RAVETTE PUBLISHING LTD
PO Box 876, Horsham, West Sussex   RH12 9GH
Tel: 01403 711443   Fax: 01403 711554   Email: info@ravettepub.co.uk
www.ravettepublishing.tel

Prices and availability are subject to change without prior notice